God the Son

by
DONALD SENIOR

Argus Communications
Allen, Texas 75002 U.S.A.

Cover photo by Jeff Wignall
Art by Jesse T. Hummingbird

Printed in the United States of America.

Argus Communications
A Division of DLM, Inc.
One DLM Park
Allen, Texas 75002 U.S.A.

International Standard Book Number 0-89505-065-X
Library of Congress Number 81-69109

0 9 8 7 6 5 4 3 2 1

Contents

Preface

Christians recognize that the story of Jesus is the story of God's Son, the light of our lives. The prime sources of that story are the Gospels, with their compelling portrayal of Jesus and his dramatic life.

Each Gospel is distinct. Mark, Matthew, Luke, and John wrote their Gospels in such a fashion that the early Christians were able to see different facets in the story of Jesus and his disciples.

Modern biblical scholars have poured over these Gospel portraits like art experts over the rarest of treasures. Each dab of color, every brush stroke and nuance of design has been studied, debated, probed. Although biblical experts differ about many things—as almost all experts tend to do—there is a remarkable consensus about the basic elements of the Jesus story.

This book is about that basic Gospel material. I do not presume that the reader has the identical interests of the biblical scholar. Analysis and dissection are needed (after all, God gave us intellects to ask why and how). But there is also a time for synthesis and reflection, because we are also people with hearts and we need to refresh our spirits. It is the latter moment this book wants to serve.

The chapters of this book center on four fundamental aspects of the Jesus story as presented in the Gospels. The first is "The World of Jesus." Archeology and refined methods of historical research have given our generation access to more information about the world in which Jesus lived than perhaps any generation since the first century itself. An awareness of the milieu in which Jesus lived breathes new meaning into the Gospel story. I have tried to present some of this information here. Jesus was God's Son, but he was also a human being, a citizen of first-century Palestine, a native of Galilee, and a devout Jew. That historical and geographical context shaped his message and his life. To know it is to know Jesus and the Gospels better.

The second chapter, "Jesus and the Kingdom," moves into the heart of Jesus' mission. Virtually every biblical scholar recognizes that the ancient Jewish hope for the coming of "God's Kingdom" was the keynote of Jesus' own ministry. Despite centuries of oppression and pain, the Jews trusted that God would ultimately deliver them and give them an experience of unending joy, peace, and security. Jesus, too, shared that hope. More than that, he was convinced that his own mission was actually to inaugurate God's Kingdom. That mission of the Kingdom encompassed all of Jesus' work: his eloquent teaching, his powerful acts of healing, his compassionate embrace of the outcast and sinner. By his ministry Jesus created a new people of God who had experienced God's life-giving rule. Each evangelist portrays Jesus' ministry in this way. John does not use the explicit terminology of the Kingdom, but his Jesus, too, is a powerful messenger of God's salvation in word and deed.

The third chapter, "Death and Victory," focuses on the climax of the Jesus story: his crucifixion and resurrection. Each of the Gospels makes these events the heart-rending yet triumphant end of the story. Death could not snuff out the light Jesus had kindled in the world. The Father raised him from the dead and in that overwhelming act of love and power gave the pledge of a new future to all humanity.

The final chapter, "To Be a Disciple," turns the spotlight to another essential and intriguing feature of the Gospels.

We can identify with the first followers of Jesus. They were ordinary people, enthralled by Jesus and his message but often baffled and capable of failure. In looking at the disciples we find ourselves and our mission.

Not unlike the original Gospel material, the contents of this book have been reshaped for new circumstances. The text and some of the illustrations are taken from a filmstrip series entitled *God the Son* (Argus Communications, 1980). Now that series has been adapted to a printed format.

The purpose remains the same: to make the Jesus of the Gospels come alive. I hope this book will provide the reader with basic information about Jesus and his message. That is why I chose to organize it around the central features of the story of Jesus as presented in the New Testament. Even more, I hope that the reflective mood of the book will serve as a source of prayer and inspiration. The Bible does not provide easy answers to our modern dilemmas, but the vision of the Scriptures is desperately needed in our troubled world. The Bible reminds us that we are sacred, that we are children of God and have reason to hope. On this foundation we might find a way to live as God's people.

Finally, it is important to note again that the pages of this book have drawn their own inspiration from the Gospels. I hope they will lead the modern reader in the same direction. There is no substitute for reading the Scriptures themselves. This book does not take the place of that encounter between the believing Christian and God's Word. Perhaps for some it can be an encouragement and a guide for discovering the beauty of the Gospels.

A final word of thanks to Jack Gargiulo and Kay Weibel of Argus Communications, whose encouragement and skill brought *God the Son* from the medium of filmstrip to the printed page.

Donald Senior

God the Son

Palestine at the time of Jesus

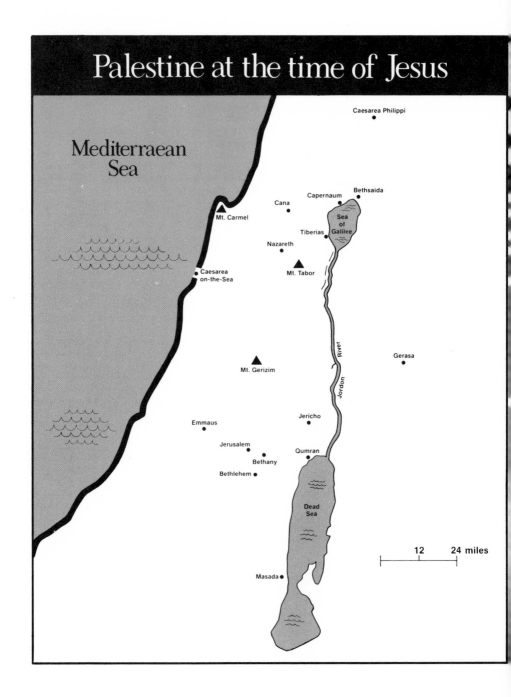

Mediterraean
Sea

Caesarea Philippi

Bethsaida
Capernaum
Cana
Mt. Carmel
Sea of Galilee
Tiberias
Nazareth
Mt. Tabor
Caesarea on-the-Sea

Jordan River

Gerasa

Mt. Gerizim

Jericho
Emmaus
Jerusalem
Qumran
Bethany
Bethlehem

Dead Sea

12   24 miles

Masada

In the beginning was the Word.
And the Word was of God,
And the Word *was* God.
And the Word became flesh and lived among us.

CHAPTER ONE

The World of Jesus

5

GOD WITH US

The mystery of our faith tells us
that Jesus is the divine son of God.
But often, it is harder
to believe the other half of the mystery . . .
that the word became *flesh*
and lived among us as one of us.

For Jesus, life on earth was filled
with divine meaning.
As he grew to manhood,
God's presence and power grew within him.
But Jesus' life also overflowed
with *human* experience and meaning.

THE BIRTH OF JESUS

Jesus was a Jew, who lived two thousand years ago
in the land we call Israel.
Like all of us,
the time and place of his birth formed the foundations
on which his life as a human person was built.

The Israel that Jesus knew
was at the crossroads
between the conquering empires
of the ancient world.
It was nestled in the fertile crescent
of the Mediterranean Sea.
Israel was at the hub of trade routes,
an oasis where goods and ideas were exchanged.

Israel's history was linked to the Jewish people,
but its population was culturally diversified,
due to centuries of Greek and Roman rule.
An educated person might even be multilingual,
speaking Greek and Latin
in addition to the native Aramaic and Hebrew.

Nature sculpted the sacred soil of Israel
into a variety of distinctive sections.
Jesus was born in Bethlehem,
a village in southern Israel,
surrounded by rugged terrain.
He lived most of his life
in the lush northern region of Galilee.

THE BOY JESUS

Jesus spent his boyhood
in the predominantly Jewish village of Nazareth.
From his earliest childhood,
he was surrounded
by the deep faith of his people.
Like all Jewish children,
he learned the Shema,
the sacred affirmation of faith,
as soon as he could speak:

"Hear O Israel: the Lord our God is One Lord;
and you shall love the Lord your God
with all your heart and with all your soul
and with all your might."

Jesus went to the synagogue each Sabbath
where he listened to readings
from the sacred scriptures,
called the Torah.

Jesus Inherited
the Jewish Tradition

Synagogue Ruins at Capernaum

Ancient Torah Archie Lieberman

Evening Prayers Garo Nalbandian

9

JESUS LEARNED THE ASTOUNDING HISTORY OF HIS PEOPLE

In ancient times, the Jews were desert nomads,
special because they followed the one God,
whom they called Yahweh.

Some migrated into the fertile Nile Delta,
to the land called Egypt,
and eventually these Israelites
were forced into Egyptian slavery.
But Yahweh raised up a mighty leader, Moses,
who led God's people out of Egypt
and to the land they would name
after their tribe, Israel.

At Mount Sinai, before reaching the promised land,
the Jews made a sacred covenant with Yahweh—
a covenant of blessings and responsibilities.
Forever, they would be his chosen people.

Later, through the prophet Isaiah,
Yahweh told his people of their destiny.
He promised them a future without death,
without tears,
without reproach from any nation on earth.

But the story of Israel's conflict and oppression
did not end with the Exodus.
Because the Jews were not always faithful
to their covenant with Yahweh,
Israel was invaded again and again.
She was often occupied by foreign powers,
her children exiled to other nations.

"How can we sing a song
to the Lord in a foreign land?" the Psalmist cried.
But then, miraculously,
the shattered dreams of the Jewish people
would be reborn.

Three centuries before the birth of Jesus,
Alexander the Great conquered the Middle East,
and for nearly two hundred years,
Israel was a vassal of the Greeks.
Finally, one Greek ruler erected a statue of Zeus
in the Holy Temple of Jerusalem.
Resentment turned to hatred.
A family of Jewish brothers known as the Maccabees
led a daring revolt,
and, against all odds, it was successful!

But all too soon,
this latest vision of freedom clouded over.
The Jewish kings became just as corrupt
as their Greek predecessors.
Jewish protest groups,
like the Pharisee party, developed.
Fearing civil war,
the leadership of Israel
called on Rome to arbitrate.
Rome came . . . and never left.

Throughout the long era of Roman domination,
the world remained in a stable,
if uneasy, peace.

By the time of Jesus' birth,
many Jews had started to dream again
of a final day of liberation.
On this day, God would raise up Israel
to her rightful place in the world.

Jesus was a Jew.
He grew up with the words of the prophets
and the dreams of his people.

Beautiful Galilee
Was Jesus' Home

Lake Galilee

Galilean Farmer

13

LIFE IN GALILEE

Although there was anxiety
and a thirst for change,
much was simple and timeless in Jesus' world—
like the beauty of the Galilean countryside.

For Jesus,
the hope and rebirth in nature
was a way of understanding and describing God's love.
Jesus used many nature images in his teaching:
the field of grain,
the birds of the air,
the one true vine,
the precious lilies of the field.

Most Galileans lived close to the land.
The multitude of peasant farmers,
called simply *Am ha' aretz,* or people of the land,
worked the soil for a meager share of the harvest.
Jesus knew these common people.
They were his friends.
Many responded and became his followers.

Other Galileans were fishermen on Lake Galilee.
With access to the world market
of the Roman Empire,
the fishing industry was prosperous in Jesus' day.
Some of Jesus' own disciples were fishermen
before he invited them
to become fishers of men.

Among Galileans living in the towns,
there were artisans, merchants,
business people, and teachers.
Jesus was called the son of a carpenter.

Every town also had its fringe element
of beggars, transients, prostitutes—
people who were usually treated
with contempt and mockery.
Jesus risked contempt himself

by openly associating with his society's outcasts
and claiming them as his friends.
"What you have done to the least of these,"
he would one day say, "you have done to me."

Most Galilean towns had a synagogue,
and the leaders of the synagogues,
called Pharisees,
were often leaders of the community as well.
Over the years,
the Pharisee party had evolved a set of codes
which defined correct and incorrect behavior.
Loyal Jews followed the codes very precisely.
This gave them a strong sense of identity
within their diversified Galilean culture.
It also made religion more practical.

Jesus traveled throughout Galilee during his ministry,
but the town to which he returned again and again
was Capernaum,
on the northwest shore of Lake Galilee.
Where silent trees now stand,
there were once alley-like streets
teeming with life.
There crowds pressed in upon Jesus—
the blind, the deaf, the crippled,
those with dreaded skin diseases.
Jesus healed all who believed.

When he visited Capernaum,
Jesus stayed at the home
of his close friend, Peter.

Jesus
Spread the Good News

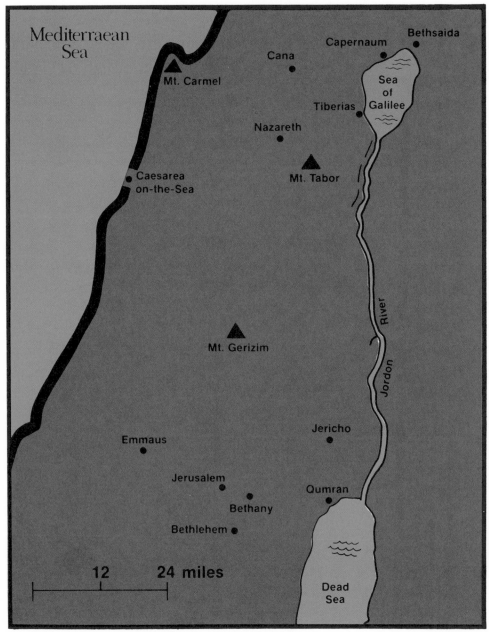

The Course of the Jordan River—A Natural Route for Travelers

The Jordan, North of Galilee   Archie Lieberman

The Dead Sea Cliffs   The Witzman Collection, The Liturgical Press

Qumran Cave   The Witzman Collection, The Liturgical Press

17

SAMARIA

Occasionally, Jesus journeyed out of Galilee
into neighboring territories.
Just south of Galilee
was the region called Samaria.
The Jews and the Samaritans
shared a common heritage,
but centuries before Jesus' birth,
the Samaritans set up
their own temple on Mt. Gerizim.
They also had their own version of the Torah.
There was a mutual distrust between
Jew and Samaritan.
But Jesus' story of the *good* Samaritan
shows that following the commandment of love
is more important than one's form of worship.

THE JORDAN RIVER

Jesus probably followed the course
of the Jordan River
in his travels from Galilee to Jerusalem.
The Jordan begins north of the Sea of Galilee
and flows south through Samaria and Judea,
spilling finally into the
salt wastes of the Dead Sea.

THE DEAD SEA

The Dead Sea is southern Israel's
only body of water.
It is also
the lowest point on the entire earth.

THE JUDEAN DESERT: A RETREAT FOR MONASTICS

It is likely that Jesus traveled farther south
into the Judean wilderness
several times in his life.
Israelites associate this desert region

with Moses and the Exodus from Egypt.
The desert symbolizes solitude, strength,
and new beginnings.
Monastics and reformers often retreated
to oasis areas in the wilderness.

THE ESSENE COMMUNITY AT QUMRAN
Jesus no doubt traveled near
the monastic community, at Qumran,
on the shores of the Dead Sea.

A Jewish reform group called Essenes
lived at Qumran.
They kept a library of scrolls
which described their way of life.
But surely in Jesus' day,
all Jews were aware of their vigil.
The Essenes lived in protest against
the Temple worship in Jerusalem,
which they viewed as corrupt.
They kept watch day and night
and prayed for the final liberation
and purification of Israel.

The Desert Temptation

Baptism Site, Jordan River

Archie Lieberr

Judean Wilderness

Donald Smetzer

21

BAPTISM AND TEMPTATION

Before beginning his ministry,
Jesus was baptized by John
in a stretch of the Jordan which winds through
Israel's barren southern half.

After his baptism, God's spirit led Jesus
into the desert wilderness of Judea
to contemplate his mission
and to be tempted by the Devil.

When Jesus had fasted for forty days
and was very hungry,
the Devil said,
"If you are the Son of God,
command these stones to become loaves of bread."

But Jesus responded, "Scripture has it,
'Man shall not live by bread alone.'"

Later, the Devil took Jesus to a high mountain
and showed him the kingdoms of the world
in all their splendor.
"All these I will give you
if you will fall down
and worship me," the Devil said.

But Jesus angrily called out
for the Devil to leave him,
avowing the sacred message of the Shema:
"You shall worship the Lord your God
and him only shall you serve."

After the Temptation
Jesus returned to Galilee
to do the work of his Father.

Jerusalem...
Where Jesus Died

Church of St. Mary Magdalene with Gethsemane Beyond

Archie Liebern

The Holy City

Archie Lieberman

JERUSALEM, THE HOLY CITY

After about three years of ministering
to the people of Galilee,
Jesus traveled up through the Judean mountains
to Jerusalem,
his nation's capital,
and the most sacred city of Judaism.

Once past the desert
he crossed the Mount of Olives.
Here the holy city bursts into full view.
On the western slope of the Mount of Olives,
just before entering the city,
is the Garden of Gethsemane.
Here Jesus prayed the night of his arrest.

Inside the city walls,
Jerusalem overflows with life, now as then.
Jesus walked amidst
the oldest portions of this city.

He taught and worshipped at the Jewish Temple,
a glorious structure in his day.
Jerusalem was the center of Israel's commerce,
and bore the image of prosperity and
international leadership.
Yet beneath the cosmopolitan surface,
Jerusalem was a tinderbox
of religious and political tensions.

POLITICAL AND RELIGIOUS DISSENSION IN JERUSALEM

The Romans kept tight control in Jerusalem.
This created tension not only between the
Romans and the general population,
but also between each group of
politically active Jews,
since each responded to Roman rule
in a different way.

The established Jewish elite,
called Sadducees,
accepted Roman rule.
From their ranks,
the Temple priests were chosen.
The Sadducees' acceptance of the Romans
caused tensions between them and the Pharisees.
The Sadducees sought to maintain
ancient Jewish ritual practices,
mostly centered in the Temple.
The Romans had little interest
in these rituals.

The Pharisees, however, wanted to make
religion more livable for the average Jew.
To do so, they sanctioned
new interpretations of scripture.
This angered the Sadducees, who
accepted only literal interpretations
of ancient Jewish law.

The militant Zealot movement
was in tension with
both the Pharisees and Sadducees.
The Zealots believed
that all Jews should take up arms
against the Roman invaders.
What they began,
God would finish.

One of Jesus' own disciples, Simon,
had probably been a member of the Zealot party.
Four disciples bore the names
of the Maccabean brothers, Simon and Judas—
a sign that revolutionary fever was high
in many Jewish households of Jesus' day.
Indeed, the Maccabees provided inspiration
for the Zealots.

Strife and Anxiety
in Jesus' World

Model of the Jerusalem Temple

Star of David Flag

Donald Smetzer

Roman Standards

R. V. Schoder. S.J.

ANXIETY FILLED THE LAND

Throughout Israel, there was a general anxiety,
a fear that things would change,
probably for the worse.
Jewish apocalyptic literature
used wild, terrifying images
to warn of an impending day of doom.

For many gentiles as well,
Roman ideals had grown stale.
Some turned to the mystical religions of the East,
whose prophets spread their ideas
throughout the Roman Empire.
In some synagogues,
special sections had to be set aside
for gentile "God-fearers,"
mostly Romans and Greeks
who had become fascinated
with the strength and consistency of Judaism.

JESUS CALLED FOR RADICAL CHANGE

A call for radical change
was also central to Jesus' message.
"Turn away from your sins," he said.
"The Kingdom of God is at hand."

So this was Jesus' world.
A world he embraced.
A world that shaped his life and message.
A world of beauty,
pain,
hope,
anxiety,
and expectation.

CHAPTER TWO

Jesus and the Kingdom

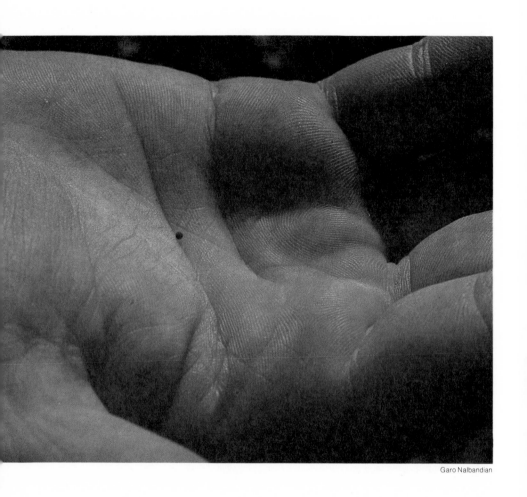

Garo Nalbandian

The Kingdom of God
is like a tiny mustard seed.
When planted in fertile earth,
it becomes the largest of plants—
a tree—where the birds of the air
can make their nests.

The Ancient Dream of a Perfect Kingdom

Egypt

Michael Haym

Mount Sinai

Jerusalem

THE TYRANNY OF EARTHLY KINGS

The idea of the Kingdom of God
was not something Jesus originated.
It was a dream whose roots went far back
into the history of his people.

The Jews had experienced Yahweh
as an all-powerful, liberator God,
who had defeated the armies
of the Egyptian Pharaoh
and allowed an oppressed people
to turn toward home.

But while the early Israelites
thought of God as their king,
they hesitated
to establish their government as a kingdom
and preferred
a loose federation of tribes instead.

They had had enough of the abuses
of earthly kings in Egypt.
They saw cruel Pharaohs maintain power by force.
They saw the fruits of monarchy:
stolen treasures,
free people turned into slaves,
great monuments erected for the glory of the king.

Samuel, one of the great prophets
of the early years,
gave an ironic list of the "rights" of a king:

"Your sons will have to plow his fields,
harvest his crops,
and make his weapons.
Your daughters will have to make perfumes for him
and work as his cooks and his bakers.
He will take your best fields,
vineyards, and olive groves,
and give them to his officials.

He will take a tenth of your flocks.
And you yourselves will become his slaves."

Eventually, though,
the Israelites did become a kingdom,
following the example of their neighbors.
Saul was selected as the first Jewish king,
and soon, Jerusalem became the capital city.

Just as Samuel predicted,
the Jewish kings turned out to be
no better than any other kings.
The history of the Jewish kings unfolded
as a history of bloodshed, battles, corruption,
and compromise of God's law.

David's Kingdom
Was Idealized

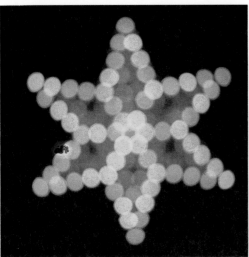

Star of David   Archie Lieberman

Fred M. Dole, Freelance Photographers' Guild
Statue of King David

Shepherd Near Bethlehem

THE SHEPHERD KING

But one Jewish king, David,
was remembered as above the rest,
as the ideal.
He was the second king,
the shepherd boy from Bethlehem.
David's rule gave the Jews
a sense of what it might be like
to really have Yahweh himself as king.
It was remembered as a time of unity,
with movement toward
justice, prosperity, and pride.

David praised God with the music of the Psalms,
and God praised David
through the words of the prophets.
Speaking through the prophet Nathan,
God promised that David's dynasty
would never end.
God would make one of David's descendants
the king of a kingdom that would last forever.

But David was human,
and he was not above corruption.
He had one of his own soldiers killed in battle
to gain the beautiful Bathsheba
for his wife.
Even so,
the Jews never forgot their shepherd king.

The Promised King of Kings

Bethlehem, the Birthplace of the Messiah

Archie Liebe

Weems Hutto

45

THE KINGDOM OF GOD IS AT HAND

In Jesus' day, many dreamed of a mighty ruler
who would lead them against the Romans
and establish a kingdom of perfect justice.
Jesus, born in Bethlehem,
was of the lineage of David.
Some of his disciples felt that he might be
the one that the prophets foretold,
the promised king of kings.

At about the age of thirty,
Jesus made a dramatic announcement
in his home village of Nazareth.
Speaking in the synagogue
where he had worshipped since childhood,
Jesus quoted from the flaming words
of the prophet Isaiah:

"The Spirit of the Lord is upon me
because he has chosen me to bring
good news to the poor.
He has sent me to proclaim liberty
to the captives
and recovery of sight to the blind,
to set free the oppressed
and announce that the time has come
when the Lord will save his people."

Following this, Jesus began to travel
throughout the towns and villages of Galilee,
proclaiming, "The Kingdom of God is at hand!"
This announcement is at the heart
of the preaching of Jesus.

But ideas about this promised Kingdom
differed greatly,
even among teachers and interpreters
who studied the scriptures constantly.
The Pharisees believed the Kingdom
belonged only to the law-abiding Jew.

Their version of the Kingdom
was tied to the notion of a perfect world,
a time in the future
when people would be rewarded
for following the law.

THE STYLE OF JESUS' MINISTRY

The Pharisees were stunned
by the style of Jesus' ministry.
It was very different from their own.
He associated with commoners, outcasts, and sinners.
He healed on the Sabbath.
He preached mercy and compassion,
and taught that the law was meant
to serve people;
people were not meant to serve the law.

The Pharisees were alarmed by the crowds
that followed Jesus.
The people followed him
because of his magnetism as a great teacher
and because he was a worker of miracles.

Jesus Used His Power to Restore Life

Cripple

Donald Smetzer

Leper

Michael Hayman

Beggar

Blind Man

49

JESUS GAVE HOPE

Jesus gave hope to the poor, healed the sick,
and gave comfort to those who mourned.
He used his power
to show that the Kingdom of God
is a *community* of love, compassion, and justice,
where God's presence empowers people
to love and serve each other.
Everywhere Jesus went,
he brought with him
the Kingdom of God.

Jesus used miracles to teach and to heal.
Lepers were outcasts
and they were forced to live outside the villages,
forbidden to go near the Temple or synagogue.
They were treated as the living dead.
Jesus touched them and healed them
and showed that they were not outcasts
in the eyes of his father.

His healing hand reached out
and gave sight to the blind.
He brought wholeness
to withered limbs and twisted minds.
Jesus did not hide from pain.

The power of his goodness
released broken bodies and broken spirits
from the evil that gripped them
and made them prisoners.
Jesus restored life.

On the hillsides of Gerasa,
across the lake from Galilee,
Jesus met a man
who was wandering around in a cemetery,
stark raving mad.
Jesus drove a host of demons
out of the man and into a herd of swine,

causing them to run down the hillside
into the lake and drown.
Because of Jesus,
this man was restored to life
from his deathlike existence.

Near the shores of Lake Galilee,
a crowd listened to Jesus.
The disciples suggested
that he send the people home
because they had followed him
for several days and they were hungry.
Instead, Jesus blessed
a few loaves of bread and fish
and fed thousands of people.
He used this miracle
to teach the importance of sharing,
just as he was sharing his whole life.

The Parables of Jesus Proclaim the Kingdom

"The Harvest Is Ready"

W. B. Finch, Stock Boston

"The One Priceless Pearl"

Michael Hayman

52

"The One True Vine"

Mark Link, S.J.

"The Good Shepherd"

Garo Nalbandian

"Look at the birds of the air," Jesus said.
"They do not plant seeds,
gather a harvest and put it in barns;
yet your Father in heaven takes care of them!
Aren't you worth much more than birds?"

Jesus taught us by his life
what God's Kingdom should be like.
He also described this Kingdom
in stories called parables
because of their symbolic meaning.
He drew these stories from the countryside
and the culture that surrounded him.

His disciples must have been startled
to hear the God of the Kingdom compared,
not to a powerful monarch,
but to an outcast—a shepherd.
Yet in one parable,
that is how Jesus described him.
If even one sheep is lost,
the God of the Kingdom, like the good shepherd,
will leave the rest of the flock
and go in search of the lost one.
And when the lost one is found,
he will hoist him on his shoulders
and bring him home rejoicing.
Ours is a God who cares,
even, and especially, for the least of us.

Or, in another story,
the Kingdom is compared
to the joy experienced by a collector of rare gems.
When he finds one really valuable pearl,
he sells everything he has
to buy the one priceless pearl.

After the resurrection,
the first Christians started preaching
about Jesus himself as the Son of God.
They realized that Jesus and his way of life

are the Kingdom of God.
Many clung to the words of urgency
in Jesus' own preaching.
The harvest is ready, keep the lamp lit,
the Kingdom of God is at hand.

But the preaching of Jesus
contains a rhythm of slow growth as well.
Jesus said the Kingdom of God is like yeast
which a woman kneads into a measure of flour.
Slowly, mysteriously, the dough begins to rise.
And more than any other symbol,
the parables of Jesus abound with images of seeds.
"This is how it is with the Kingdom," he said.
"A man scatters seed on the ground.
Day after day, he goes to bed and gets up,
and growth seems slow.
Yet finally it does grow,
without his knowing how it happened."

ENTERING THE KINGDOM

To enter the Kingdom,
we must become new people.
The Gospel calls it *"metanoia"*—
a change of heart.
The transformation is still in process.
It depends completely on us
and (here is the mystery)
it also depends completely on God.
Our hearts are converted
when we let part of ourselves die
so that God *can* transform us into new persons.
So, the everlasting new life of the Kingdom
is both in us and growing through us.

CHAPTER THREE

Death and Victory

Pat Hallett-Korn

57

This is where the story of Jesus of Nazareth ends.
This is where the story of Christianity begins.

Death Seems So Final

Pat Hallett-Korn

Road from Jerusalem to Emmaus

61

Death seems so final.
How are hope and faith possible
amidst pain and death?

Haunted by thoughts such as these,
two disciples of Jesus fled Jerusalem
in shock and despair three days after his death.
As they walked toward the nearby village of Emmaus,
they discussed the whirlwind of events
that preceded the crucifixion.

JESUS PROVED HIS POWER OVER DEATH BY RAISING LAZARUS

A few weeks before Jesus was to celebrate the Passover,
he received word that one of his closest friends,
Lazarus,
had died in Bethany, just outside Jerusalem.
Jesus went to the home of his friend
and found that he had already been buried
for four days.
Jesus called Lazarus out of his tomb.
Soon, crowds of people,
anticipating the Passover celebrations,
started to gather in Jerusalem.
When they heard about Lazarus,
they wanted to meet and question the man
who Jesus had raised from death.
After seeing the evidence
of Jesus' power over death,
many believed in him.
Others, however, went straight back
to the religious authorities and told them
about this man performing all sorts of signs.
The leaders were frightened.
"If we let him go on thus," they said,
"everyone will believe in him,
and the Romans will come and destroy
both our holy place and our nation."

JESUS ENTERED JERUSALEM TRIUMPHANTLY

Some of the disciples asked Jesus
if he intended to go to Jerusalem
for the Passover festival.
The people were stirred up.
The authorities were plotting to kill him.
The situation seemed dangerous.
But Jesus went to the Holy City anyway.

"Hosanna!" the people cried.
"Blessed is he who comes in the name of the Lord!"
"Blessed is the kingdom
of our father David that is coming!
Hosanna in the highest!"

But Jesus did not lead a glorious rebellion
against the Romans.
He did not take the crown of Israel.
Instead, he continued that same style of ministry
he had brought to the towns of Galilee.

JESUS SPOKE ABOUT HIS DEATH

Jesus patiently tried to prepare the disciples
for the events that would take place.
"The Son of Man must suffer much and be rejected
by the elders, the chief priests,
and the teachers of the Law.
He will be put to death,
but three days later
he will rise to life again."
Sometimes he spoke to the people in parables.
"Unless a grain of wheat falls
to the earth and dies,
it remains alone.
But if it does die, it bears much fruit."

The Passion

Citadel of David, Probable Site of Jesus' Trial

Archie Lieberm

Garden of Gethsemane

The disciples could not believe
that Jesus would suffer or die a violent death.
He was always surrounded by eager, expectant crowds.
He embodied that merciful and renewing
surge of life
that Israel had always hoped for from its God.
He drove the merchants and money-changers
from the Temple courtyard,
and claimed the Jerusalem Temple for his Father.
Every day he taught in the Temple.
He healed the crippled,
and gave sight to the blind.
Always, through his words and actions,
he put compassion and mercy
above every other obligation.
The authorities did not dare apprehend Jesus
in front of the crowds he taught and healed.

JESUS' FAREWELL MEAL

Then, the night before he died,
Jesus had a last supper with the twelve.
Again he spoke about his death.
"I am going to prepare a place for you," he said.
He offered them broken bread and a cup of wine
as signs of a new bond between God and his people.

After supper, Jesus went to his prayer retreat,
the Garden of Gethsemane.
As he sat beneath the ancient olive trees,
his soul filled with despair.
He knew that the hour he had predicted
was upon him.
But Jesus loved life.
He did not want to die.
Crushed by grief,
he begged his Father to take away this suffering.
"Yet not what I want, but what you want," he prayed.

Meanwhile, the disciples who came
with Jesus to the garden
had fallen asleep from sorrow and exhaustion.

ARREST, INTERROGATION, CRUCIFIXION: IT ALL HAPPENED SO QUICKLY

Soon, a party of soldiers came to arrest Jesus.
Immediately, his followers
began to scatter in fear.
By dawn, even Peter had denied three times
that he knew Jesus.
Throughout the night,
Jesus was led from place to place and interrogated:
First, he was questioned by the Jewish council,
then by Pilate, the Roman governor of Judea,
then by King Herod of Galilee
who was in town for the Passover,
and finally back to Pilate again.
Herod had been eager
to meet the famed miracle worker from Nazareth,
but Jesus refused to perform
any signs to save himself.

HE COULD NOT SAVE HIMSELF

The next morning,
Jesus staggered through the streets of Jerusalem,
carrying the crossbeam
on which he would be nailed.
The hostile crowds threw insults at him.
His power and charisma seemed gone.
To those along the path,
he was no wonder worker now.
The sign above his head bore the initials for his crime
in Hebrew, Greek, and Latin:
"Jesus of Nazareth, King of the Jews."
The authorities ridiculed Jesus,
"He saved others; he cannot save himself."

Resurrection:
A Promise Kept

Travelers on the Road to Emmaus

Garo Nalbandian

The Empty Tomb

Lew Gordon

THE WALK TO EMMAUS

Because of the finality of all that
happened in Jerusalem,
two of Jesus' disciples had left for Emmaus.
Their leader was dead.
The community of followers had dispersed,
and many were hiding,
in fear for their lives.

As they walked along,
a third person caught up to them
and asked what they were talking about.
They were amazed
that he did not already know.
"Are you the only visitor in Jerusalem
who doesn't know the things
that have been happening
there these last few days?"
"What things?" he asked.
"The things that happened to Jesus of Nazareth,"
they answered.
"This man was a prophet
and was considered by God and by all the people
to be powerful in everything he said and did.
Our chief priests and rulers
handed him over to be sentenced to death,
and he was crucified.
And we had hoped that he would be the one
who was going to set Israel free!"

THE PROPHESIES FORETOLD ALL THIS

The third traveler reproached the disciples
for their slowness to believe.
He began to explain the scriptures
and they felt a fire burning inside them.

These scriptures testify
that the God of Israel, Yahweh,
is a god of *life* and *rebirth*.
This is the God described by Ezekiel,

who had a dream
in which he was taken to a desert place
filled with dried and bleached bones.
Yahweh poured out his breath on the bones,
and the spirit of life entered them.
They joined together and took on flesh.
Yahweh said to Ezekiel,
"Prophesy to my people Israel
and tell them that I, the Lord God,
am going to open their graves.
I am going to take them out
and bring them back to the land of Israel.
When I open the graves where my people are buried
and bring them out,
they will know that I am the Lord."

The third pilgrim challenged the disciples
for their lack of understanding about the Messiah.
Didn't they know it was necessary
for him to suffer before coming into his glory?
The prophet Isaiah plainly foretold this:
"But he endured the suffering
that should have been ours,
the pain that we should have borne.
All the while we thought that his suffering
was punishment sent by God.
But because of our sins he was wounded,
beaten because of the evil we did.
We are healed by the punishment he suffered,
made whole by the blows he received."
They drew near to Emmaus,
but the disciples wanted to hear more.

The Cross:
A Symbol of Victory

Pat Hallett-Korn

Jeff Wignall

They urged the third traveler
to remain with them for supper.
As their mysterious friend broke the bread,
they recognized him as Jesus
and he disappeared immediately.
"It is the Lord!" they exclaimed.
Their hearts filled with joy.
"He is risen!"
Immediately, they got up and returned to Jerusalem.
The city they left
had seemed shrouded in darkness and despair.
But when they returned
to the community of followers,
they began to hear of other encounters
between the risen Jesus and those who loved him.

HE IS RISEN!
The women who had gone to anoint Jesus' body
found the tomb empty.
As they stumbled back out on the road,
there he was waiting to greet them!
Filled with joy and victory,
they ran to tell the others, "He is risen!"
Some disciples were hiding in an upper room,
terribly afraid and in deep despair.
Suddenly Jesus was with them,
eating their food,
giving them peace and strength.
Other disciples, tense and depressed,
had returned to their work
as fishermen on Lake Galilee,
but they caught nothing.
Then someone on the shore suggested
where they might drop their nets.
The voice and the calm authority were familiar.
"It is Jesus!"

But he is also different.
He comes and goes mysteriously,
and is hard to recognize at first.

The incredible has happened.
Jesus is transformed into new life.
Nothing of Jesus would be snuffed out by death.
His teaching on love was not a fantasy.
His compassion for the poor and for the outcasts
was not an empty gesture.
His commitment to justice was not futile.
His trust in the Father was not in vain.
The hoped-for has come true.
The Father has raised Jesus from the dead!

The cross was the dreaded fate
of the convicted criminal.
But Christians have made it
into a symbol of victory.
Why?

Because sacrifice, suffering, and death,
even a humiliating and painful death,
did not defeat Jesus,
and they do not have to defeat us either.
The only bridge
between life on earth and life everlasting
is the power of God and our faith in him.

For Christians, this means faith
in the resurrection and the promise of Jesus.
We are a resurrection people.
Jesus promises us new vitality
in living out our commitment to love one another.
We can hope for a new future of joy and reunion.

Jesus said, "I am the resurrection and the life.
Whoever believes in me will live,
even though he dies;
and whoever lives and believes in me
will never die."

CHAPTER FOUR

To Be a Disciple

Don Doll, S.J.

77

"Follow me,
And I will make you become fishers of men."

The First Disciples: Ordinary People

Arab Man

Archie Lieberman

Garo Nalbandian

81

Most leaders of great movements enter history
as bigger than life.
They are immortalized in paintings and monuments,
and we tend to remember them as perfect beings.

The founding leaders of the Christian community
were chosen by Jesus to build the Kingdom.
He loved them
and empowered them to do everything he did.
But were they in fact extraordinary and holy people?
Were they bigger than life?
Not according to the Gospels.
The Gospels communicate clearly
that the disciples were, like ourselves,
very human.
They never really understood Jesus.
And when it came to the crisis,
one betrayed him,
and the rest denied and deserted him.
How could these men
have become the disciples of Jesus
and launched the most powerful
movement in history?

FROM ALL WALKS OF LIFE

Some of the first called were fishermen.
Smoked and pickled fish
were exported all over the Roman Empire,
and to own some boats on the Sea of Galilee
made one comfortable middle class.

Passing along by the Sea of Galilee,
Jesus saw Simon Peter
and his brother Andrew casting a net.
"Follow me," he said,
"and I will make you become fishers of men."

Soon afterward, Jesus saw a man named Matthew
sitting at the tax office.
Tax collectors were normally despised

by pious Jews.
They helped the Romans drain Israel
of its own wealth.
But Jesus called Matthew,
and the tax man rose up and followed.

Another disciple, Simon,
was a political revolutionary,
a member of the group which was determined
to overthrow the Roman occupation by force.

Two others, James and John,
were nicknamed *Boanerges*,
literally "hot heads."

And what we don't know
about most of the other disciples says even more:
Philip; Thaddaeus; James, son of Alpheus;
Thomas; Bartholomew—
they are a faceless blur in history.

DISCIPLESHIP: IN JESUS' DAY,
THE COMMON WAY TO LEARN

Discipleship was a system
the Jews inherited from the Greeks.
It was the accepted form
of Jewish education in Jesus' day.
It was then typical for a rabbi, or teacher,
and his students to be together constantly.
They lived and studied together
until the disciples
were ready to become rabbis themselves.

Jesus and his disciples
were also together constantly,
but among the followers of Jesus,
there were no graduates.

Jesus told his disciples,
"One among you is your teacher,
the rest are learners."

Under the ancient system,
a disciple always chose his rabbi,
and with the greatest of care.
But the disciples of Jesus did *not* choose him.
He chose them.

CHOSEN, DESPITE WEAKNESS AND FAILURE

Jesus knew that the disciples were *not* heroes.
So why did he choose them to be his followers?
He picked them precisely because they were ordinary,
not bigger than life,
but representative of life.

All of the disciples had commonplace weaknesses.
They seemed slow to understand.
They missed the significance
of Jesus' healing power.
They were baffled by his parables.

They were selfish and ambitious
and wanted personal glory.
They even argued among themselves
about who was the "greatest."

They were petty and lacked generosity.
When Jesus proposed to feed hungry crowds,
the disciples urged
that they be sent away without food.
When parents brought their children
to Jesus to be blessed,
the disciples told them not to bother the master.
They were jealous of each other
and of anyone outside their group
who began to teach and heal in Jesus' name.

But the disciples were sometimes
worse than unheroic.
The very name of one disciple, Judas,
has become a synonym for "traitor."
And Judas was not the only failure.

Others slept through Jesus' agony
in the Garden of Gethsemane
when he asked them to watch.
They all finally bolted and ran
when armed soldiers came to arrest Jesus.
And while Jesus was on trial,
Peter, to whom Jesus had entrusted
the keys of the Kingdom,
denied throughout the night
that he even knew his Galilean master.
At the end, only a few women
and the faithful disciple,
John, remained with Jesus.

So, the Gospels portray the disciples
as real people
who had the incredible privilege
of being chosen by Jesus to spread his community.
He had confidence in them

and empowered them to serve others
and to perform signs.
But these privileges
came in spite of weakness and failure.

O MAN OF LITTLE FAITH

One vivid scene dramatizes
this human image of the disciples.
They are caught in a storm on the Sea of Galilee,
foundering about in a small boat.
Suddenly, Jesus himself comes to rescue them,
walking upon the mighty sea.
Peter is awed and thrilled by the power of the moment.
He cried out to Jesus,
asking to share in his mastery over storm and sea.
Incredibly, his wish is granted.
"Come," says Jesus.

But soon,
Peter senses the power of the wind and the sea.
He is afraid,
he loses heart,
and he begins to sink.
"O man of little faith,"
Jesus says as he reaches out
to rescue his panic-stricken friend.
Because of Jesus the storm is calmed,
and Peter is saved,
as are all the other disciples.
If the disciples *had* been overwhelmed
by defeat and failure,
the Gospels would not be
the story of good news.

RECONCILIATION OVERCOMES FAILURES

At the last supper, Jesus told the disciples,
"All of you will lose faith in me,
but after I am raised up
I will go back to Galilee ahead of you."

Jesus promised to restore the bond
between himself
and those he knew would desert him,
and he did.

On a hilltop in Galilee,
the risen Jesus appeared
to his confused and broken-hearted disciples.
To seal his forgiveness for their failure,
he commissioned them to preach the good news
to the whole world.

Over a breakfast by the sea,
Peter's threefold denial was fully healed
by a threefold pledge of love
which the glorified Jesus drew from his disciple:

"Simon Peter, do you love me?"
"Lord, you know everything,
you know that I love you."
And Peter, too, was restored
to his mission: "Feed my sheep."

Jesus also appeared to many of his other followers,
among them the two disillusioned disciples
who were walking from Jerusalem to Emmaus.
Jesus was a mysterious pilgrim to them at first—
walking with them, interpreting the scriptures.
But all of a sudden,
when he broke the bread,
they knew who he was
and everything made sense.

Contemporary Disciples

Burk Uzzle, Magnum Photos

Weems H

Ken Firestone

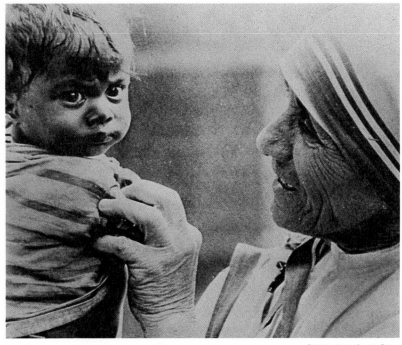

Religious News Service Photo

WE WHO BELIEVE

We who believe in Jesus
have much the same experience
as the first disciples.
As Christians we are called to follow him
and carry forward his mission.

We hear the teaching of Jesus,
we learn about his miracles,
and we are told about his Kingdom.
But the story of Jesus makes sense only
when we experience for ourselves
the light beyond light and
the power beyond power
which only belief can bring.

LOVE ONE ANOTHER

Jesus challenges us to love and heal one another.
"By the love you have for one another,
everyone will know you are my disciples."
This doesn't mean
that we will never experience
the suffering and failure
of the first disciples.

We all know what it means
to be selfish rather than giving,
to be indifferent
rather than compassionate and loving.
But the ultimate message of the Gospel
is forgiveness and new life.

Our ways are not God's ways.
Jesus knows that we are human,
in need of support and encouragement.
He helps us see reality through the eyes of faith.
The power of Jesus comes to us
in many mysterious ways—
sometimes in a moment of peace at prayer.

We feel his presence
in the bond of friendship and love,
and in the promise
that love does not come to an end.

We find his inspiration and encouragement
when we gather to worship as Christians,
when we read or hear
the healing word of the scriptures,
when we share the bread and cup of the Lord,
and when we carry forward the mission of Jesus
to serve others:

"Whatever you do for the least of
my brothers and sisters, you do for me."

We are Christians, called to follow Jesus,
to learn from him,
to share in his life,
to serve others in his name.
Our call is an invitation
to continue Jesus' work in the world,
each in response to the talents
that have been given us.
We are called to heal as Jesus healed,
to teach as Jesus taught,
to challenge the forces of evil,
and to work for social justice and human growth.

Robert McKendrick

92

"Lord, make me an instrument of your peace,
where there is hatred, let me sow love;
where there is injury, pardon;
where there is doubt, faith;
where there is despair, hope;
where there is darkness, light;
and where there is sadness, joy.

Grant that I may not so much seek
to be consoled as to console;
to be understood as to understand;
to be loved as to love.

For it is in giving that we receive;
it is in pardoning that we are pardoned;
and it is in dying
that we are born into eternal life."

ABOUT THE AUTHOR

Donald Senior is a native of Philadelphia and teaches New Testament in the Chicago Cluster of Divinity Schools. He was ordained in 1967 and received his doctorate in biblical studies from the University of Louvain in Belgium in 1972. Since then, he has published seven books on Scripture and numerous articles in scholarly and popular journals. He has hosted several T.V. series on the Bible in the Chicago area.

Don Senior's work revolves around the Bible and people. He has lectured on Scripture throughout the United States, Canada, the Far East, Australia, and Africa. Last year, Don Senior taught in a special Bible program in Jerusalem. "I'm grateful," he says, "for having had the chance to teach in several parts of the world. It was an opportunity to meet new people and see new places but, even more, it taught me the power of God's Word. The Masai of Tanzania, Korean students in Seoul and urban dwellers in Chicago have at least one thing in common: they can all catch fire when they come in contact with the meaning of the Scriptures. The Bible belongs to the people."

Besides writing, lecturing, and teaching, he also confesses to being an avid baseball fan (an infection left over from his own playing days in college) and a bemused observer of the political scene. Two interesting hobbies to have in Chicago!